South Dakota

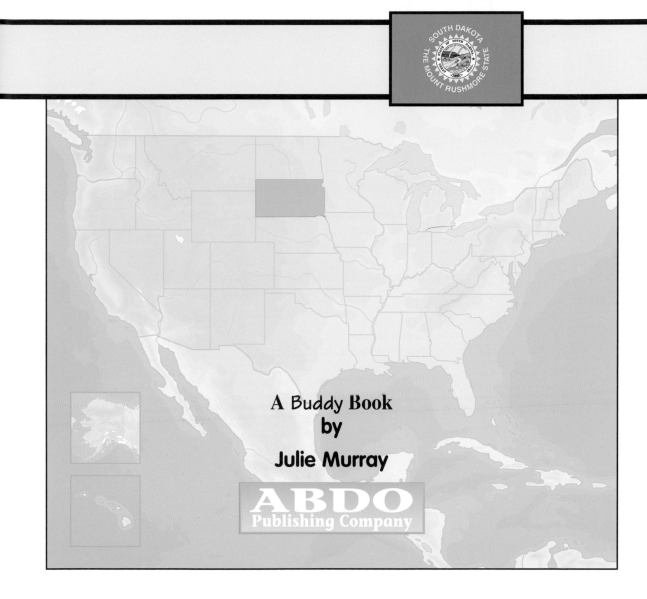

A Buddy Book
by
Julie Murray

ABDO
Publishing Company

VISIT US AT

www.abdopub.com

Published by ABDO Publishing Company, 4940 Viking Drive, Edina, Minnesota 55435.

Copyright © 2006 by Abdo Consulting Group, Inc. International copyrights reserved in all countries. No part of this book may be reproduced in any form without written permission from the publisher. Buddy Books™ is a trademark and logo of ABDO Publishing Company.

Printed in the United States.

Edited by: Sarah Tieck
Contributing Editor: Michael P. Goecke
Graphic Design: Deb Coldiron, Maria Hosley
Image Research: Sarah Tieck
Photographs: Ben Mueller, Clipart.com, Creatas, Digital Vision, Getty Images, Library of Congress, One Mile Up, Photodisc

Library of Congress Cataloging-in-Publication Data

Murray, Julie, 1969-
   South Dakota / Julie Murray.
      p. cm. — (The United States)
   Includes bibliographical references and index.
   ISBN 1-59197-700-2
      1. South Dakota—Juvenile literature. I. Title.

F651.3.M87 2005
978.3—dc22

2005048115

Table Of Contents

A Snapshot Of South Dakota

South Dakota is known for its landmarks and scenery. The Black Hills and the Badlands are there. Many people travel to South Dakota to see its landscape.

There are 50 states in the United States. Every state is different. Every state has an official nickname. South Dakota is known as "the Mount Rushmore State." It is home to Mount Rushmore. This is a famous sculpture that honors past presidents.

A view of the Badlands
in South Dakota.

South Dakota became the 40th state on November 2, 1889. Today, South Dakota is the 16th-largest state in the United States. It has 77,122 square miles (199,745 sq km) of land. South Dakota is home to 754,844 people.

Custer State Park is in the Black Hills of South Dakota.

Where Is South Dakota?

There are four parts of the United States. Each part is called a region. Each region is in a different area of the country. The United States Census Bureau says the four regions are the Northeast, the South, the Midwest, and the West.

South Dakota is in the Midwest region of the United States. The geographical center of all 50 states is in South Dakota. It is 17 miles (27 km) west of Castle Rock. There is a marker there to show the exact spot.

Four Regions of the United States of America

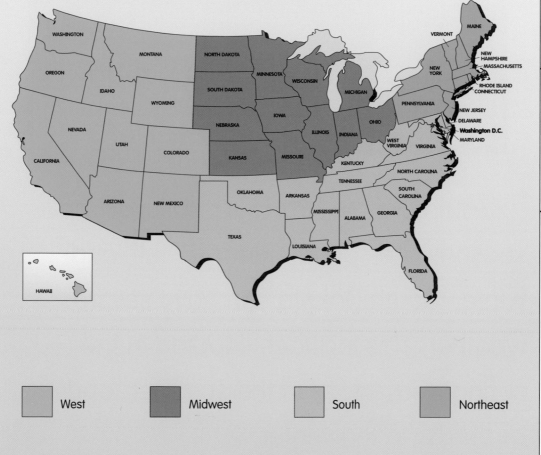

West   Midwest   South   Northeast

Sometimes, there are storms during the summer months.

South Dakota has four seasons. The seasons are spring, summer, fall, and winter. South Dakota can have severe weather. This includes flooding in the spring, tornadoes in the summer, and blizzards in the winter.

South Dakota is bordered by six other states. North Dakota is north. Minnesota and Iowa are east. Nebraska is south. Wyoming and Montana are west.

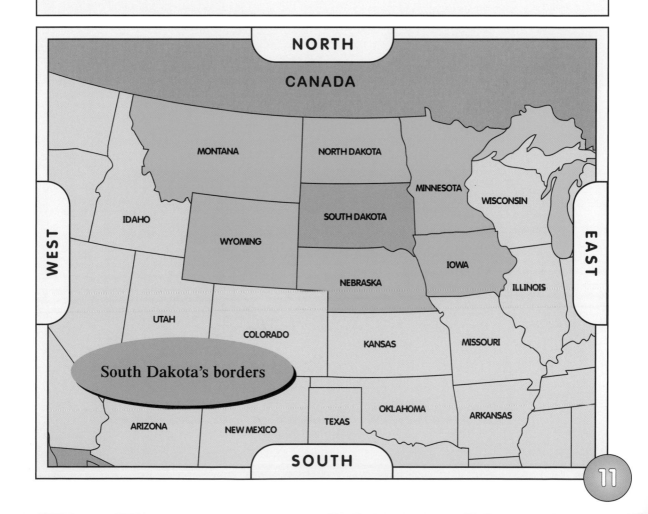

South Dakota

State abbreviation: SD

State nickname: The Mount Rushmore State

State capital: Pierre

State motto: Under God the People Rule

Statehood: November 2, 1889, 40th state

Population: 754,844, ranks 46th

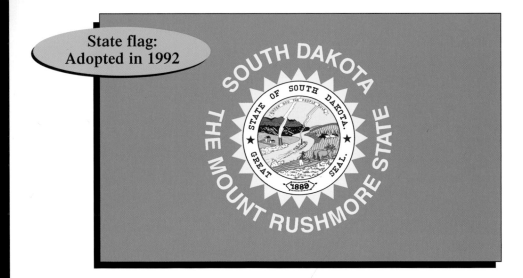

State flag:
Adopted in 1992

Land area: 77,122 square miles (199,745 sq km), ranks 16th

State song: "Hail, South Dakota"

State government: Three branches: legislative, executive, and judicial

Average July temperature: 74°F (23°C)

Average January temperature: 16°F (-9°C)

State flower:
American pasqueflower

State animal:
Coyote

State bird:
Ring-necked pheasant

Cities And The Capital

Pierre is the **capital** city of South Dakota. Pierre is located in the center of the state along the Missouri River. It was named for Pierre Chouteau. He was a French fur trader.

South Dakota's State Capitol.

The Corn Palace in Mitchell

Sioux Falls is the largest city in South Dakota. It has many businesses. It is near the falls of the Big Sioux River. This is where the city got its name.

The city of Mitchell is 60 miles (97 km) west of Sioux Falls. The famous Corn Palace is located in Mitchell. The outside of the building is a mural made of corn, grains, and grasses.

Famous Citizens

Tom Brokaw (1940–)

Tom Brokaw was born in Webster in 1940. He is a famous reporter. He is best known for his work in television. He was the anchor of *NBC Nightly News* from 1982 to 2004. He has also written several books.

Tom Brokaw

Famous Citizens

Tom Daschle (1947–)

Tom Daschle was born in Aberdeen in 1947. Daschle served in the United States House of Representatives starting in 1979. He became a United States Senator in 1987. He is best known for his work to help South Dakota's farmers. Daschle also served as the leader of the Democratic Party in the Senate. Daschle left the Senate in 2005 when he lost re-election.

Tom Daschle

Native Americans

Native Americans are a large part of South Dakota's history. They have lived in South Dakota for thousands of years. Early Native American tribes lived off the land. They hunted animals such as bison. They also grew crops such as corn and squash.

There were several main Native American tribes that lived in South Dakota. The Arikara, Cheyenne, and Sioux are among these tribes.

Native Americans and U.S. officials at the Pine Ridge Indian Reservation.

When settlers arrived in South Dakota in the mid-1800s, they tried to take the land where the Native Americans lived. The Native American tribes fought to keep their land. But they lost this battle, and the United States Government forced them to live on reservations.

In South Dakota, the Native Americans' battle continued for many more years. In 1973, Native Americans occupied Wounded Knee on the Pine Ridge Indian Reservation for 71 days. They did this to help get better treatment from the United States government.

South Dakota's Landscape

Some famous landscapes are found in South Dakota. One of these areas is the Black Hills. Another is the Badlands.

The Black Hills are found in the southwestern part of the state. These are low mountains covered with thick forests. People travel to the Black Hills to see rock formations, streams, and scenery. Harney Peak is found there. It is the highest point in South Dakota. It stands 7,242 feet (2,207 m) high. This is also where Mount Rushmore is located.

The Badlands are famous for unusual rock formations.

The Badlands are also found in southwest South Dakota. This area has rolling grasslands. But, the Badlands are not grasslands. This unusual landscape is made from sandstone and clay. The rock formations and hills change colors and shapes. This is because of the wind and rain.

Mount Rushmore

The Mount Rushmore National Memorial is a famous United States monument. Mount Rushmore is in the Black Hills of South Dakota. It honors four great United States presidents. They are George Washington, Thomas Jefferson, Theodore Roosevelt, and Abraham Lincoln.

Mount Rushmore
National Memorial

Mount Rushmore was built by Gutzon Borglum. It is one of the world's largest sculptures. Each face is 60 feet (18 m) tall.

Construction began on Mount Rushmore in 1927. Borglum hired about 400 people. Only some of them worked on the mountain. Others built roads to the monument, sharpened tools, or helped out in other ways. Working on Mount Rushmore was full of danger. Yet, only a couple of people were hurt and nobody died.

It took 14 years to build Mount Rushmore. Today, more than 2 million people visit Mount Rushmore every year. The park is free and open all year.

The faces of four presidents are carved into Mount Rushmore.

Mount Rushmore is in the Black Hills of South Dakota.

South Dakota

1682: René-Robert Cavelier, Sieur de La Salle, claims South Dakota for France.

1803: President Thomas Jefferson arranges for the United States to buy South Dakota as part of the Louisiana Purchase.

1804: Meriwether Lewis and William Clark begin to explore South Dakota.

1861: Congress creates the Dakota Territory.

1863: The Dakota Territory opens for homesteading. Many settlers arrive.

1889: South Dakota becomes the 40th state on November 2. North Dakota becomes the 39th state on the same day.

1890: Hundreds of Native Americans are killed near Wounded Knee Creek. This happens after they surrender to the United States Army. This will later be called the Massacre of Wounded Knee.

A memorial for the people who died at Wounded Knee

1927: Gutzon Borglum begins work on Mount Rushmore.

1989: South Dakota celebrates its centennial.

2004: Events throughout South Dakota honor the bicentennial of Lewis and Clark's exploration of the state.

Cities In South Dakota

Important Words

bicentennial 200-year anniversary.

blizzard a heavy snowstorm with strong winds.

capital a city where government leaders meet.

centennial 100-year anniversary.

Louisiana Purchase a deal where the United States bought land from France. Part of this land later became South Dakota.

nickname a name that describes something special about a person or a place.

reservation public land set aside for Native Americans to live on.

sculpture a piece of art formed from stone, wood, metal, or other matter.

tornado a storm cloud that is shaped like a funnel and swirls fast, destroying homes and cities.

Web Sites

To learn more about South Dakota, visit ABDO Publishing Company on the World Wide Web. Web site links about South Dakota are featured on our Book Links page. These links are routinely monitored and updated to provide the most current information available.

www.abdopub.com

Index